Safety First

by Rebecca Weber

Content Adviser: September Kirby, CNS, MS, RN,
Instructor, Health Promotion and Wellness,
South Dakota State University

Reading Adviser: Rosemary G. Palmer, Ph.D.,
Department of Literacy, College of Education,
Boise State University

Spyglass
BOOKS

COMPASS POINT BOOKS

Minneapolis, Minnesota

Compass Point Books
3109 West 50th Street, #115
Minneapolis, MN 55410

Visit Compass Point Books on the Internet at *www.compasspointbooks.com*
or e-mail your request to *custserv@compasspointbooks.com*

Photographs ©: Tom Stewart/Corbis, cover; Stockbyte, 4, 10, 17; Norbert Schaefer/Corbis, 5;
Corbis, 6; Brand X Pictures, 7, 12, 13, 15, 18; Paul Osmond/Deep Sea Images, 8; Digital Vision, 9;
PhotoDisc, 11, 20 (bottom), 21 (top); Comstock, 14; Unicorn Stock Photos/Aneal O. Vohra, 16;
Creatas, 19; Image Library, 20 (top), 21 (bottom).

Editor: Patricia Stockland
Photo Researcher: Marcie C. Spence
Designer: Jaime Martens

Library of Congress Cataloging-in-Publication Data
Weber, Rebecca.
  Safety first / by Rebecca Weber.
     p. cm. — (Spyglass books)
  Includes index.
  Summary: Introduces the concept of safety, providing examples of how to be safe
at home, in school, while traveling, and on the playground.
  ISBN 0-7565-0626-3 (hardcover)
  1. Safety education—Juvenile literature. 2. Children's accidents—Prevention—
Juvenile literature. [1. Safety.] I. Title. II. Series.
  HQ770.7.W433 2004
  613.6'083—dc22   2003014471

Contents

NOTE: Glossary words are in **bold** the first time they appear.

Staying Safe

When you know how to stay safe, you can have a lot of fun.

Look Before You Leap

Before you do anything, just think about it. Could it hurt you or anyone else?

Safe at Home

Think about your house.
Is it safe? The stove can
get hot. There are sharp
knives. There may be
pills or cleaning *solutions*
that can make you sick.

Ouch!

Even your nice, soft bed can be unsafe. If you jump on your furniture, you could fall off and break a bone.

You can help make your home a safe place.

Go from room to room with an adult. Ask her to *label* anything that might be *poisonous.* Have her throw away any old medicine.

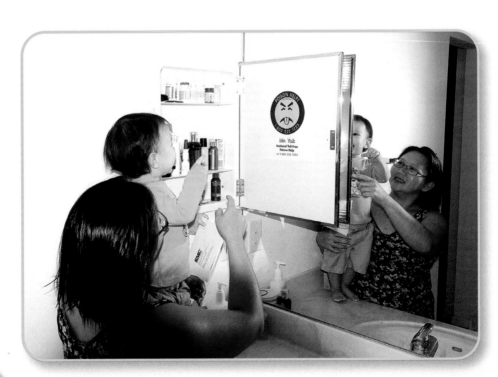

Helpful Hint

Never eat or drink anything without asking an adult if it is OK.

Safe at School

Think about your school. Is it safe? People who are running can crash into each other. Spilled food can make the floor slippery.

You can make your school a safe place.

Don't run in the halls. Make sure that no one runs into you. In gym class, pay attention to the rules.

Visitors to the School

Never go anywhere with an adult you do not know. If a stranger asks for your help, find a teacher who can help instead.

Field Trip Fun

When you go on a field trip, stay with the group. You will have more fun. You won't get hurt or lost.

Safe on the Road

Think about when you go someplace. Is it safe?

Cars may have **accidents.** You could fall off your bicycle. You could even get lost.

Protect Your Head

If you ride a scooter, a skateboard, or a bike, always wear a helmet. **15**

You can make your travel time safe. Always wear a seatbelt. If you are walking or riding, look out for cars. They may not see you, so you have to watch for them.

Helpful Hint

If you ride a bus, always stay in your seat when the bus is moving. When you get off the bus, look for cars before you cross the road. **17**

Playing It Safe

Think about your playground. Is it safe?

Follow the rules, and everyone will stay safe.

Swimming Safe

Never swim alone. If something happens to one person, the other can go for help. Remember, safety first!

Fire Drill

Many schools have fire drills. You can have a fire drill at home.

 Figure out two ways you could escape from your home.

Plan where everyone in the family will meet when they are outside the building.

 Know what telephone numbers you should call for help once you are safe.

 Practice the fire drill. See how long it takes everyone to get out safely. Practice until everyone knows what to do.

Glossary

accident-when something goes wrong or something gets broken

label-to mark something with a sign that says what it is

poisonous-something that can make a person or animal very sick

solutions-liquids or mixtures

Learn More

Books

Dewan, Mohit, and Disha Dewan.
*Safety First: An Activity Book
for Kids.* Rochester, Minn: Lone
Oak Press, 1996.

Silverstein, Alvin. *Staying Safe.*
New York: Franklin Watts, 2000.

On the Web

For more information on
Safety First, use FactHound
to track down Web sites related
to this book.
1. Go to *www.compasspointbooks.com/
facthound*
2. Type in this book ID: 0756506263
3. Click on the *Fetch It* button.
Your trusty FactHound will fetch
the best Web sites for you!

Index

GR: J
Word Count: 199

From Rebecca Weber

The world is such a great place! I love teaching kids how to take care of themselves and take care of nature.